quilts, bibs, blankies... oh my!

CREATE YOUR OWN CUTE & CUDDLY NURSERY

Kim Schaefer

C&T PUBLISHING

Text copyright © 2008 by Kim Schaefer

Artwork copyright © 2008 by C&T Publishing, Inc.

Publisher: Amy Marson

Editorial Director: Gailen Runge

Acquisitions Editor: Jan Grigsby

Editor: Lynn Koolish

Technical Editors: Carolyn Aune and Helen Frost

Copyeditor: Wordfirm Inc.

Cover Designer/Book Designer: Kristen Yenche

Production Coordinator: Tim Manibusan

Illustrator: Richard Sheppard

Photography by Luke Mulks and Diane Pedersen of C&T Publishing Inc., unless otherwise noted

Published by C&T Publishing, Inc., P.O. Box 1456, Lafayette, CA 94549

Library of Congress Cataloging-in-Publication Data

Schaefer, Kim.

    Quilts, bibs, blankies-- Oh my! : create your own cute & cuddly nursery / Kim Schaefer.

        p. cm.

    Summary: "Collections of quilts and other small projects to make for babies and toddlers"--Provided by publisher.

    ISBN 978-1-57120-491-2 (paper trade : alk. paper)

    1. Quilting--Patterns. 2. Machine appliqué--Patterns. I. Title.

    TT835.S2843 2008

    746.46'041--dc22

2007031650

Printed in China

10 9 8 7 6 5 4 3

DEDICATION

To my babies, Cody, Ali, Max, Ben, Sam, and Gator. No matter how you grow or where you go, you will always be my babies.

ACKNOWLEDGMENTS

I feel so fortunate to work with C&T Publishing. Although my name is on the cover, I am just one part of the team that put this book together. The entire staff is talented, professional, and a pleasure to work with.

Special thanks to: Lynn Koolish, my editor, for making the whole process so easy and rewarding. Caroline Aune and Helen Frost, my technical editors. Caroline and Helen have the huge job of checking and rechecking the accuracy of all the patterns. Thank you for being so thorough and correcting my mistakes. Kristen Yenche for the great cover and book design. Kristen is such a talented designer, her work gives the book its lighthearted personality. Finally, thank you to Richard Sheppard for the exceptional illustrations.

Thanks to:

Lynn Helmke, for her beautiful and creative machine quilting. Lynn quilted all the crib quilts, wall quilts, and growth charts featured in this book.

My husband, Gary Schaefer, for everything, including his superior computer knowledge and skills.

Andover/Makower fabrics for the supply of great fabrics.

A great big thank you to Chris Jeske for her fine handwork. Chris sewed the bindings on many of the quilts, and she has helped me with my work for many years. The quality of her workmanship is unsurpassed, whether it be piecing, cutting, or binding.

contents

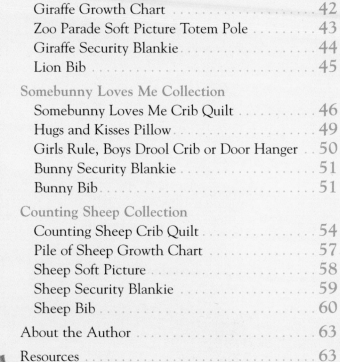

introduction

There is nothing quite like the joy and excitement that the arrival of a new baby brings, and no better way to celebrate the occasion than with a special gift that is handmade with love. As babies, all of my six children had a favorite quilt or blanket that brought comfort, warmth, and a sense of security and that was literally loved to pieces.

Whether you are a first-time sewer or an experienced quilter, there are projects in this book that are appropriate for your skill level. The designs use machine appliqué and simple piecing techniques. There are six collections, each featuring a different theme. Each collection has a crib quilt and coordinating accessories. There are wall quilts, growth charts, pillows, soft pictures, and crib or door hangers to decorate the nursery. The security blankies are done in cuddly soft Minkee, Flurr, and flannel (specialty fabrics readily available at your local quilt shop) and are the perfect size for snuggling and going anywhere and everywhere with baby. Each collection also has a bib design—a simple and fun gift perfect for every baby.

I hope that in the following pages you will find the perfect gift idea to welcome your new little one with love.

general directions

ROTARY CUTTING

I recommend that you cut all the fabrics used in the pieced blocks, borders, and bindings with a rotary cutter, an acrylic ruler, and a cutting mat. Trim the blocks and borders with these tools as well.

PIECING

All piecing measurements include ¼″ seam allowances. If you sew an accurate ¼″ seam, you will have happiness, joy, and success in quilting. If you don't, you will have misery, tears, and the seam ripper.

PRESSING

Press seams to one side, preferably toward the darker fabric. Press flat, and avoid sliding the iron over the pieces, which can distort and stretch them. When you join two seamed sections, press the seams in opposite directions so you can nest seams and reduce bulk.

APPLIQUÉ

All the appliqué instructions are for fusible web with machine appliqué. If you prefer a different appliqué method, you will need to add seam allowances to the appliqué pieces.

Appliqué patterns have been drawn in reverse. A lightweight paper-backed fusible web works best for machine appliqué. Choose your favorite fusible web, and follow the manufacturer's directions.

General Appliqué Instructions

1. Trace all parts of the appliqué design on the paper side of the fusible web. Trace each layer of the design separately. Whenever two shapes in the design butt together, overlap them by about ⅛″ to help prevent the potential for a gap between them. When tracing the shapes, extend the underlapped edge ⅛″ beyond the drawn edge in the pattern. Write the pattern letter or number on each traced shape.

2. Cut around the appliqué shapes, leaving a ¼″ margin around each piece.

3. Iron each fusible web shape to the **wrong** side of the appropriate fabric. Cut on the tracing lines, and peel the paper backing off the fusible web. A thin layer of fusible web will remain on the wrong side of the fabric—this will adhere the appliqué pieces to the backgrounds.

4. Position the pieces on the backgrounds. Press to fuse in place.

5. Machine stitch around the appliqué pieces using a zigzag, satin, or blanket stitch. Stitch any other lines on the patterns to add detail.

CUTTING TRIANGLES

Some of the projects use half-square triangle blocks (see *Cars, Buses, Trucks, and Trains Crib Quilt* on page 17). Because the quilts are scrappy, I usually cut the triangles from squares and sew them together individually. I always make more than I need so that I have choices when assembling the quilt top. In each project I give exact measurements used in that quilt. If you want to change the size of the blocks, it is important to know the basic formula for making half-square triangles. The cut size of the half-square triangle square equals the finished block size plus ⅞″. For example, if you need a 6″ finished block, cut the squares 6⅞″ × 6⅞″. Cut the squares in half diagonally once to make two triangles. The instruction for this is "cut squares on the diagonal."

Cut squares on diagonal.

Other triangles will be created by cutting squares diagonally twice to create quarter-square triangles. The instruction for this is "cut squares diagonally twice." The formula for the cut size of a quarter-square triangle square is the finished block size plus 1¼″.

Cut squares diagonally twice.

PUTTING IT ALL TOGETHER

When all the blocks are completed for a quilt, lay them out on the floor or, if you are lucky enough to have one, a design wall. Arrange and rearrange the blocks until you are happy with the overall look of the quilt. Each project has specific directions, as well as diagrams and photos, for assembling the top.

BORDERS

If the quilt borders need to be longer than 40″, join crosswise strips of fabric together at a 45° angle as necessary, and cut the strips to the desired length. All borders in the book are straight cut (no mitered corners).

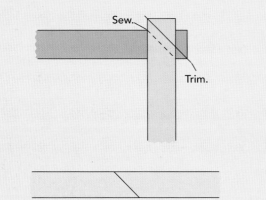

LAYERING THE QUILT

Cut the batting and backing pieces 2″ to 3″ larger than the quilt top. Place the pressed backing on the bottom, right side down. Place the batting over the backing and the quilt top on top, right side up. Make sure all the layers are flat and smooth and the quilt top is centered over the batting and backing. Pin or baste the quilt.

QUILTING

Quilting is a personal choice; you may prefer hand or machine quilting. My favorite method is to send the quilt top to a longarm quilter. This method keeps my number of unfinished quilt tops low and the number of finished quilts high.

COLOR AND FABRIC CHOICES

I have used 100% cotton fabrics in all the quilts, growth charts, wall quilts, pillows, and soft pictures in this book. The security blankies are made with some of the great new fabrics such as Minkee and Flurr, as well as flannel, which are all available at your local quilt shop. They are so soft and cuddly, it's hard to stop touching them. You may want a blankie of your own.

TIP
Minkee and Flurr are stretchy fabrics. Take care when cutting them.
Flurr is also very messy. Once the fabric is cut, little pieces of Flurr fuzz are everywhere. As soon as you bind the Flurr, the mess stops; so bind quickly. The snuggle factor of this fabric makes it worth the mess.

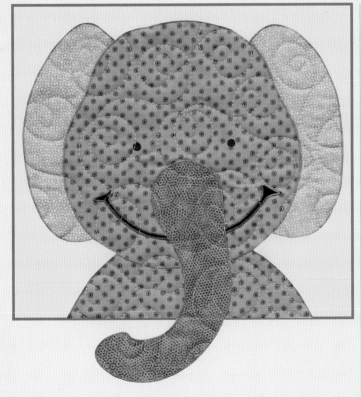

MAKING THE QUILT YOUR OWN

If you want to change the size of a quilt, simply add or subtract blocks or change the width of the borders. Feel free to enlarge or reduce the appliqué patterns. Your color choices may be totally different from mine.

YARDAGE AND FABRIC REQUIREMENTS

I have given yardage and fabric requirements for each project, many calling for a total amount of assorted fabrics that can be used as a base for your quilt. The yardage amounts may vary depending on several factors: the size of quilt, the number of fabrics used, and the number of pieces you cut from each fabric.

I prefer to use the lengthwise grain of the fabric for quilt backing, even on smaller projects. For larger quilts, I piece together two or three lengths of fabric.

Binding fabric amounts allow for 2″-wide strips cut on the straight of grain. Strips are cut on the bias for projects with curved edges. Fusible web amounts are based on a 17″ width.

I have used both traditional and not-so-traditional color choices for the quilts and other projects. Today's nurseries are not always done in the soft pastels that have traditionally been thought of as baby colors; many nurseries today are bright and bold. The *Moon and Stars* collection (page 8) and the *Somebunny Loves Me* collection (page 46) both use traditional soft pastels. Other collections use bright fabrics. The *Counting Sheep* collection (page 54) features primarily black and white fabrics with little touches of brightly colored fabrics. For the first few weeks of life, babies see only in black and white and high contrast. Although this combination is not necessarily traditional, it stimulates a baby's development.

Thankfully, everyone has different tastes when it comes to color. Whether you prefer pastels or brights or something in-between, any design can be adapted to your preference.

You can give baby the moon and stars with this sweet collection, which includes a crib quilt, pillow, soft picture, door or crib hanger, security blankie, and bib. This collection, which is great for a baby shower, features easy appliqué shapes and super-simple piecing.

moon and stars crib quilt

Quilted by Lynn Helmke

Finished block size: 6″ × 6″

Finished crib quilt size: 42½″ × 54½″

CUTTING

Cut 18 squares $6\frac{1}{2}'' \times 6\frac{1}{2}''$ from assorted yellows for appliqué block backgrounds.

Cut 21 squares $6\frac{1}{2}'' \times 6\frac{1}{2}''$ from assorted blues for appliqué block backgrounds.

Cut 72 rectangles $2\frac{1}{2}'' \times 6\frac{1}{2}''$ from assorted blues for pieced border.

APPLIQUÉ BLOCKS

Refer to Appliqué on page 5.

1. Trace and cut out 18 stars (#1) and 21 moons (#2). (Appliqué patterns are on pages 15–16.)

2. Appliqué the appropriate pieces onto the backgrounds.

3. Draw or embroider faces on the stars.

Star block, make 18.

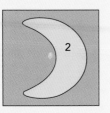

Moon block, make 21.

PUTTING IT ALL TOGETHER

Refer to the diagram below.

Blocks

1. Arrange and sew together the appliqué blocks in 7 rows of 5 blocks each. Press.

2. Sew together the rows to form the quilt top. Press.

Borders

1. Arrange and sew together 2 sets of 21 rectangles $2\frac{1}{2}'' \times 6\frac{1}{2}''$ to form the side borders.

2. Sew the side borders to the quilt top. Press.

3. Arrange and sew together 2 sets of 15 rectangles $2\frac{1}{2}'' \times 6\frac{1}{2}''$ to form the top and bottom borders. Press.

4. Sew an appliquéd moon block to each end of the top and bottom borders.

5. Sew the top and bottom borders to the quilt top. Press.

Finishing

1. Layer the quilt top with batting and backing, and baste or pin.

2. Quilt as desired, and bind.

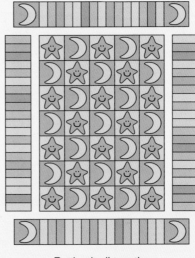

Putting it all together

MATERIALS

- $1\frac{1}{2}$ yards total assorted yellows for appliqué block backgrounds and moons

- $2\frac{1}{2}$ yards total assorted blues for appliqué block backgrounds, stars, and pieced border

- $3\frac{5}{8}$ yards for backing and binding

- 3 yards paper-backed fusible web

- $46'' \times 58''$ batting

- Black permanent fabric marker or embroidery floss for star faces

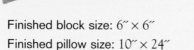

star pillow

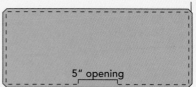

Finished block size: 6″ × 6″
Finished pillow size: 10″ × 24″

MATERIALS

- ¼ yard total assorted yellows for appliqué block backgrounds
- ⅜ yard total assorted blues for sashing, borders, and appliquéd stars
- ⅓ yard blue for pillow back
- ¼ yard paper-backed fusible web
- Polyester fiberfill
- Black permanent fabric marker or embroidery floss for faces

CUTTING

Cut 3 squares 6½″ × 6½″ from assorted yellows for appliqué block backgrounds.

Cut 2 rectangles 1½″ × 6½″ from assorted blues for sashing.

Cut the following from assorted blues for border strips:

1 strip 1½″ × 20½″ for border 1

1 strip 1½″ × 7½″ for border 2

1 strip 1½″ × 21½″ for border 3

1 strip 1½″ × 8½″ for border 4

1 strip 1½″ × 22½″ for border 5

1 strip 1½″ × 9½″ for border 6

1 strip 1½″ × 23½″ for border 7

1 strip 1½″ × 10½″ for border 8

Cut 1 rectangle 10½″ × 24½″ from blue for pillow back.

APPLIQUÉ BLOCKS

Refer to Appliqué on page 5.

1. Trace and cut out 3 stars (#1). (The appliqué pattern is on page 15.)

2. Appliqué the stars onto the backgrounds. (Refer to the Star block diagram on page 9.) Make 3.

3. Draw or embroider faces on the stars.

PUTTING IT ALL TOGETHER

1. Follow the border sequence numbers, and sew the borders onto the pillow top clockwise, pressing toward the border after each addition.

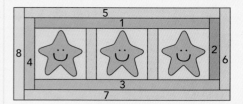

Add borders.

2. With right sides together, sew the pillow front to the pillow back, leaving a 5″ opening at the bottom of the pillow for stuffing. Trim the seam allowances to ⅛″ at the pillow corners.

Trim corners.

5″ opening

Sew pillow front to pillow back.

Finishing

1. Turn the pillow right side out.

2. Stuff the pillow with polyester fiberfill.

3. Finish the seam on the bottom of the pillow by hand stitching it closed.

wake him…take him door or crib hanger

Finished block size: 6″ × 6″
Finished hanger size: 10″ × 10″

MATERIALS

- ⅛ yard total assorted yellows for center block and appliquéd moon
- ⅛ yard total assorted blues for border and appliquéd stars
- 10½″ × 10½″ blue for hanger back
- ⅛ yard paper-backed fusible web
- 1⅜ yards ⅞″-wide blue grosgrain ribbon for hanger
- Polyester fiberfill
- Black permanent fabric marker or embroidery floss for faces and lettering

CUTTING

Cut 3 rectangles 2½″ × 6½″ from assorted yellows for center block.

Cut the following from assorted blues for border strips:

1 strip 2½″ × 6½″ for border 1

1 strip 2½″ × 8½″ for border 2

1 strip 2½″ × 8½″ for border 3

1 strip 2½″ × 10½″ for border 4

Cut 2 pieces 24″ long from ribbon.

PIECING

1. Sew together the 3 yellow rectangles to form the center block. Press.

2. Follow the border sequence numbers, and sew the borders onto the center block clockwise, pressing toward the border after each addition.

APPLIQUÉ

Refer to Appliqué on page 5.

1. Trace and cut out 3 small stars (#3) and 1 small moon (#4). (Appliqué patterns are on page 15.)

2. Appliqué the appropriate pieces onto the hanger.

3. Write or embroider the lettering. (The pattern is on page 16.) Replace "Him" with "Her" if you are making the hanger for a girl. Draw or embroider the star faces.

PUTTING IT ALL TOGETHER

1. Pin the grosgrain ribbon to the front of the hanger 1″ in from both ends, with the long ends of the ribbon facing toward the center of the hanger.

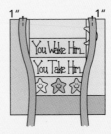

2. Pin the long ends of the ribbon away from the edges of the hanger so the ribbon will not get caught in the seam. With right sides together, sew the hanger front to the hanger back, leaving a 4″ opening at the bottom of the hanger for stuffing. Trim the seam allowances to ⅛″ at the hanger corners.

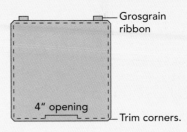

Sew hanger front to hanger back.

Finishing

1. Turn the hanger right side out.

2. Stuff the hanger with fiberfill.

3. Finish the seam on the bottom of the hanger by hand stitching it closed.

4. Tie the ends of the grosgrain ribbon in a knot about 6″ from the stuffed hanger. Tie a bow on top of the knot.

star soft picture

MATERIALS

- ¼ yard yellow for appliqué block background
- ¼ yard total assorted blues for border and appliquéd star
- 10½″ × 10½″ blue for back
- ¼ yard paper-backed fusible web
- ½ yard ⅞″-wide blue satin ribbon for hanger
- 10½″ × 10½″ batting
- Black permanent fabric marker or embroidery floss for star face

CUTTING

Cut 1 square 6½″ × 6½″ from yellow for appliqué block background.

Cut the following from assorted blues for border strips:

    1 strip 2½″ × 6½″ for border 1

    1 strip 2½″ × 8½″ for border 2

    1 strip 2½″ × 8½″ for border 3

    1 strip 2½″ × 10½″ for border 4

Cut 1 piece 15″ long from ribbon.

APPLIQUÉ

Refer to Appliqué on page 5.

1. Trace and cut out 1 star (#1). (The appliqué pattern is on page 15.)

2. Appliqué the star onto the background. (Refer to the Star block diagram on page 9.)

3. Draw or embroider the star face.

PIECING

Follow the border sequence numbers, and sew the borders onto the appliqué block clockwise, pressing toward the border after each addition.

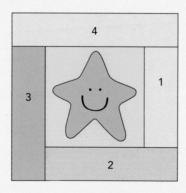

Add borders.

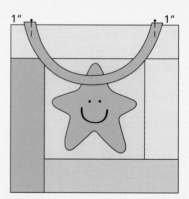

Finished soft picture size: 10″ × 10″

PUTTING IT ALL TOGETHER

1. Layer quilt batting under the picture front. Quilt as desired.

2. Position and pin the ends of the blue satin ribbon 1″ in from the sides of the picture. Place the shiny side of the ribbon facing the front of the soft picture.

Pin ribbon to picture front.

3. With right sides together, sew the picture front to the picture back, leaving a 4″ opening at the bottom of the picture for turning. Trim the seam allowances to ⅛″ at the picture corners.

Finishing

1. Turn the picture right side out. Press.

2. Finish the seam on the bottom of the picture by hand stitching it closed.

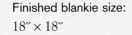

moon security blankie

CUTTING

Cut 1 square 18″ × 18″ from yellow Flurr for blankie.

Cut 2¾″-wide bias strips from the yellow flannel, and piece them end-to-end to make a 74″ strip for binding.

Make a template of pattern piece 5 (page 15). Place the template on the corners of the blankie, and cut the corners.

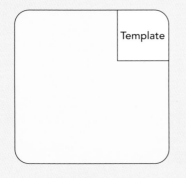

Cut blankie corners.

APPLIQUÉ

Refer to Appliqué on page 5.

1. Trace and cut out 1 moon (#2). (The appliqué pattern is on page 16.)

2. Appliqué the moon onto the blankie.

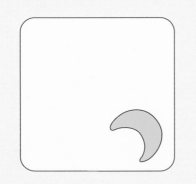

Appliqué moon onto blankie.

PUTTING IT ALL TOGETHER

1. Fold the flannel binding strip in half lengthwise with the wrong sides together, and press flat.

2. Pin and sew the strip to the front of the blankie with the raw edges together, using a ¼″ seam. Stop a few inches before the end, fold under the end of the strip, and trim the excess. Overlap the folded end over the beginning, and finish stitching in place.

Folded end

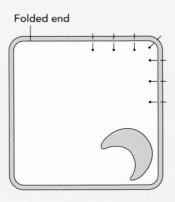

Sew binding to blankie.

Finishing

Turn the folded edge of the binding strip around to the back of the blankie, and hand stitch in place.

MATERIALS

- ⅝ yard yellow Flurr for blankie

- ½ yard yellow flannel for binding

- ¼ yard yellow for appliquéd moon

- ¼ yard paper-backed fusible web

- Template plastic (optional)

Finished blankie size: 18″ × 18″

star bib

Finished bib size: 8″ × 11½″

APPLIQUÉ

Refer to Appliqué on page 5.

1. Trace and cut out 1 star (#1). (The appliqué pattern is on page 15.)

2. Appliqué the star onto the bib.

3. Draw or embroider the face.

Appliqué star onto bib.

MATERIALS

- ⅓ yard white terry cloth
- ¼ yard blue for appliquéd star
- ¼ yard blue for bias binding or 1 package of purchased bias tape
- ¼ yard paper-backed fusible web
- 1″ × 2″ piece sew-in hook-and-loop tape
- Black permanent fabric marker or embroidery floss for face
- Template plastic (optional)

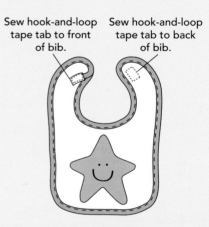

CUTTING

Copy the bib pattern, and flip it over to make both halves of the bib. (The pattern is on the pullout.) Make a template of the complete bib. Place the template on the terry cloth. Mark and cut the bib background.

If you are making bias binding, cut bias strips 1¼″ wide from the blue, and piece them end-to-end as necessary to make 49″ of bias binding.

PUTTING IT ALL TOGETHER

1. Fold and press ¼″ on each side of the bias strip along the length of the strip.

2. Fold the strip in half lengthwise, pressed edges together.

3. Sew the binding to the bib, ⅛″ from the folded edges, starting at the upper left corner.

Start here.

Sew binding to bib.

4. Overlap the edge of the binding strip at the starting point, and sew the hook-and-loop tape in place. The loop portion of the tape will cover the free end of the binding strip.

Sew hook-and-loop tape tab to front of bib.

Sew hook-and-loop tape tab to back of bib.

Sew hook-and-loop tape to bib.

1

Star

4

Small moon

Security blankie corner

5

Corner template

3

Small star

You Wake Him...
You Take Him...

Saying

Her

Alternate word

2

Moon

He (or she) can take his wheels wherever he goes when you make him one of the projects featured in the *Cars, Buses, Trucks, and Trains* collection. Make a crib quilt, a train wall quilt, a car soft picture, a car security blankie, and a train engine bib.

cars, buses, trucks, and trains crib quilt

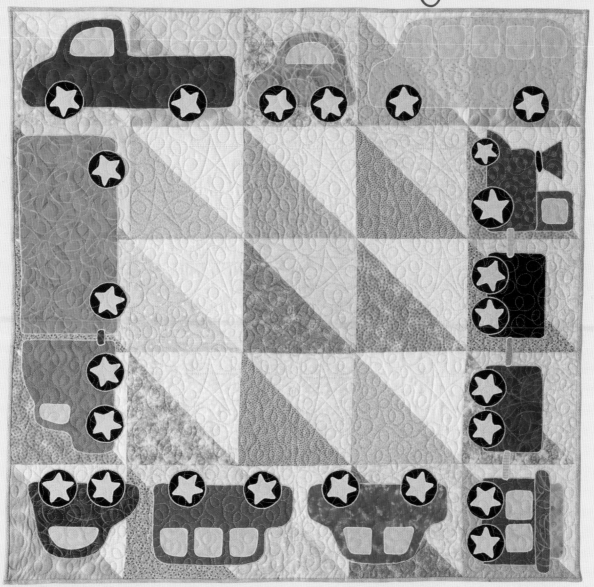

Quilted by Lynn Helmke

Finished block size: 8″ × 8″

Finished crib quilt size: 40½″ × 40½″

CUTTING

Cut 13 squares $8\frac{7}{8}'' \times 8\frac{7}{8}''$ from assorted light blues for pieced blocks; cut squares on the diagonal to yield 26 triangles (refer to page 5). You will use 25 of the triangles.

Cut 13 squares $8\frac{7}{8}'' \times 8\frac{7}{8}''$ from assorted medium blues for pieced blocks; cut squares on the diagonal to yield 26 triangles. You will use 25 of the triangles.

PIECED BLOCKS

Sew together a light blue triangle and a medium blue triangle on the diagonal edges. Press toward the medium blue triangle. Make 25 blocks.

Piece blocks, make 25.

PUTTING IT ALL TOGETHER

Refer to the diagram below.

Piecing

1. Arrange and sew together the pieced blocks in 5 rows of 5 blocks each. Press.

2. Sew together the rows to form the quilt top. Press.

Appliqué

Refer to Appliqué on page 5.

1. Trace and cut out the appliqué pieces (appliqué patterns are on the pullout). Make 22 star hub caps (#1) and 22 wheels (#2). Make 3 train hitches (#9). Make 2 small cars and 2 small train cars. Make 1 each of all the other pieces.

2. Appliqué the pieces onto the quilt top.

Finishing

1. Layer the quilt with batting and backing, and baste or pin.

2. Quilt as desired, and bind.

MATERIALS

- 1 yard total assorted light blues for pieced blocks and appliquéd windows

- 1 yard total assorted medium blues for pieced blocks

- 1¼ yards total assorted brights for appliqué pieces

- ¼ yard black for wheels

- ⅛ yard white for star hub caps

- 1¾ yards for backing and binding

- 3 yards paper-backed fusible web

- 44″ × 44″ batting

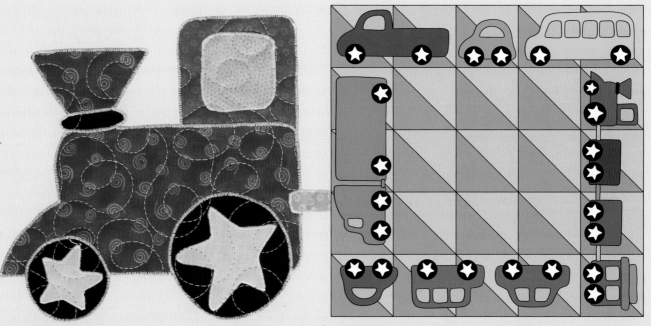

Putting it all together

train wall quilt

Quilted by Lynn Helmke

Finished block size: 6″ × 6″
Finished wall quilt size: 30½″ × 12½″

CUTTING

Cut 4 squares 6½″ × 6½″ from light blue for appliqué block backgrounds.

Cut 24 squares 3½″ × 3½″ from medium blues for pieced border.

PIECING

Arrange and sew together the appliqué block backgrounds in 1 row of 4 blocks. Press.

APPLIQUÉ

Refer to Appliqué on page 5.

1. Copy the train engine, small train car, and caboose patterns on the pullout at 75% size. Trace and cut out the reduced appliqué pieces. Make 3 train hitches (#9), 6 star hub caps (#1), and 6 wheels (#2) for the cars and caboose. Make 2 small train cars and 1 each of the other pieces.

2. Appliqué the appropriate pieces onto the background.

Appliqué pieces onto background.

PUTTING IT ALL TOGETHER

Refer to the diagram below.

Pieced Border

1. Sew together 2 rows of 8 squares for the top and bottom borders. Press. Sew the top and bottom borders to the quilt top. Press toward the center.

2. Sew together 2 rows of 4 squares for the 2 side borders. Press. Sew the side borders to the quilt top. Press.

Finishing

1. Layer the quilt with batting and backing, and baste or pin.

2. Quilt as desired, and bind.

Putting it all together

car soft picture

MATERIALS

- ¼ yard light blue for appliqué block background
- ¼ yard total assorted medium blues for pieced border
- ⅛ yard red for car
- ⅛ yard white for star hub caps
- ⅛ yard black for tires
- Small scrap of light blue for window
- 10½″ × 10½″ for back
- ¼ yard paper-backed fusible web
- ½ yard ⅞″-wide blue gros-grain ribbon for hanger
- 10½″ × 10½″ batting

Finished soft picture size: 10″ × 10″

CUTTING

Cut 1 square 6½″ × 6½″ from light blue for appliqué block background.

Cut the following from assorted medium blues:

    1 strip 2½″ × 6½″ for border 1

    1 strip 2½″ × 8½″ for border 2

    1 strip 2½″ × 8½″ for border 3

    1 strip 2½″ × 10½″ for border 4

Cut 1 piece 15″ long from ribbon.

APPLIQUÉ

Refer to Appliqué on page 5.

1. Copy the small car pattern on the pullout at 75% size. Trace and cut out the reduced appliqué pieces (#1–#3).

2. Appliqué the appropriate pieces onto the background.

Appliqué car onto background.

Refer to the directions in Piecing and Putting It All Together on page 12 to finish the soft picture.

car security blankie

CUTTING

Cut 2 squares 18″ × 18″ from blue Minkee for blankie front and back.

Refer to Cutting on page 13 for corners and binding.

APPLIQUÉ

Refer to Appliqué on page 5.

1. Copy the small car pattern on the pullout at 75% size. Trace and cut out the reduced appliqué pieces (#1–#3).

2. Appliqué the car onto the blankie front.

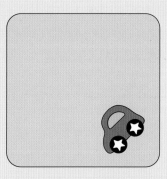

Appliqué car onto blankie front.

Refer to the directions in Putting It All Together on page 13 to finish the blankie.

Finished blankie size: 18″ × 18″

train engine bib

MATERIALS

- ⅓ yard white terry cloth for bib
- ¼ yard total of 2 reds for engine
- ⅛ yard white for star hub caps
- ⅛ yard black for tires and engine piece
- Small scrap of blue for window
- ¼ yard blue for bias binding or 1 package of purchased bias tape
- ¼ yard paper-backed fusible web
- 1˝ × 2˝ piece sew-in hook-and-loop tape
- Template plastic (optional)

Finished bib size: 8˝ × 11½˝

CUTTING

Copy the bib pattern, and flip it over to make both halves of the bib. (The pattern is on the pullout.) Make a template of the complete bib. Place the template on the terry cloth. Mark and cut the bib background.

If you are making bias binding, cut bias strips 1¼˝ wide from the blue, and piece them end-to-end as necessary to make 49˝ of bias binding.

APPLIQUÉ

Refer to Appliqué on page 5.

1. Copy the train engine pattern on the pullout at 75% size. Trace and cut out 1 each of reduced pieces #1–#8.

2. Appliqué the train engine onto the bib.

Appliqué train engine.

Refer to the directions in Putting It All Together on page 14 to finish the bib.

Starfish and Friends Collection

Decorate baby's nursery with this great collection of aquatic friends. The collection includes the *Starfish and Friends Crib Quilt*, a fish pillow, a turtle soft picture, a starfish security blankie, and a frog bib.

starfish and friends crib quilt

Quilted by Lynn Helmke

Finished block size: 8″ × 8″

Finished crib quilt size: 34½″ × 52½″

MATERIALS

- 1¼ yards light turquoise for appliqué block backgrounds

- ½ yard blue for sashing strips

- ⅛ yard dark blue for sashing squares

- 1½ yards total assorted jewel tones for appliqué pieces and pieced border

- ¼ yard black for mouths

- ⅛ yard white for eyes

- 2 yards for backing and binding

- 2 yards paper-backed fusible web

- 38″ × 56″ batting

- Black permanent fabric marker or embroidery floss for eyes

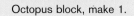

CUTTING

Cut 15 squares 8½″ × 8½″ from light turquoise for appliqué block backgrounds.

Cut 38 rectangles 1½″ × 8½″ from blue for sashing strips.

Cut 24 squares 1½″ × 1½″ from dark blue for sashing squares.

Cut 160 rectangles 1½″ × 3½″ from assorted jewel tones for pieced border.

APPLIQUÉ

Refer to Appliqué on page 5.

1. Trace and cut out the appliqué pieces. (Appliqué patterns are on pages 31–38.) Make 7 starfish and 1 each of the other sea creatures.

2. Appliqué the appropriate pieces onto the backgrounds.

3. Draw or embroider the pupils in the eyes.

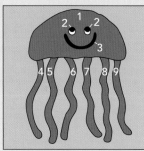

Jellyfish block, make 1.

Starfish block, make 7.

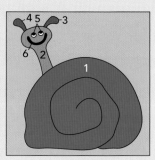

Snail block, make 1.

Octopus block, make 1.

Frog block, make 1.

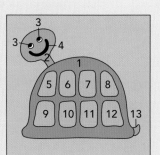

Sea horse block, make 1.

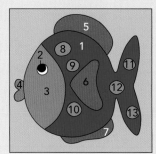

Fish block, make 1.

Crab block, make 1.

Turtle block, make 1.

PUTTING IT ALL TOGETHER

Refer to the diagram at right.

Piecing

1. Arrange the appliqué blocks into 5 rows of 3 blocks each.

2. Sew the sashing strips between the blocks. Press toward the sashing.

Sew sashing strips between appliqué blocks.

3. Sew together 3 sashing strips and 4 sashing squares in a row. Press toward the sashing. Make 6.

Sew sashing strips, make 6.

4. Sew the block rows between the sashing strip rows. Press.

Pieced Border

1. Arrange and sew together 2 sets of 46 rectangles 1½″ × 3½″ to form the side borders. Press.

2. Sew the side borders to the quilt top. Press toward the sashing.

3. Arrange and sew together 2 sets of 34 rectangles 1½″ × 3½″ for the top and bottom borders. Press.

4. Sew the top and bottom borders to the quilt top. Press toward the sashing.

Finishing

1. Layer the quilt with batting and backing, and baste or pin.

2. Quilt as desired, and bind.

Putting it all together

fish pillow

Finished block size: 8″ × 8″
Finished pillow size: 16″ × 16″

MATERIALS

- ⅓ yard light turquoise for appliqué block background

- ⅝ yard blue for sashing strips and pillow back

- ⅛ yard dark blue for sashing squares

- ⅓ yard total assorted jewel tones for appliqué pieces and pieced border

- Scrap of white for eye

- 2 yards purchased purple piping

- ¼ yard paper-backed fusible web

- 16″ × 16″ pillow form

- Black permanent fabric marker or embroidery floss for eye

CUTTING

Cut 1 square 8½″ × 8½″ from light turquoise for appliqué block background.

Cut the following from blue:

    4 strips 1½″ × 8½″ for sashing strips

    2 rectangles 11″ × 16½″ for pillow back

Cut 4 squares 1½″ × 1½″ from dark blue for sashing squares.

Cut 52 rectangles 1½″ × 3½″ from assorted jewel tones for pieced border.

APPLIQUÉ

Refer to Appliqué on page 5.

1. Trace and cut out the fish appliqué pieces (#1–#13). (The appliqué pattern is on page 36.)

2. Appliqué the appropriate pieces onto the background. (Refer to the Fish block diagram on page 24.)

3. Draw or embroider the pupil of the eye.

PUTTING IT ALL TOGETHER

Refer to the diagram on page 27.

Sashing Border

1. Sew a sashing strip to opposite sides of the appliqué block. Press toward the sashing.

2. Sew a sashing square to each end of the remaining 2 sashing strips. Press toward the sashing.

3. Sew the top and bottom sashing strips to the block. Press toward the sashing.

Pieced Border

1. Arrange and sew together 2 sets of 10 rectangles 1½″ × 3½″ for the side borders. Press.

2. Sew the side borders to the pillow front. Press toward the sashing.

3. Arrange and sew together 2 sets of 16 rectangles 1½″ × 3½″ for the top and bottom borders. Press.

4. Sew the top and bottom borders to the pillow front. Press toward the sashing.

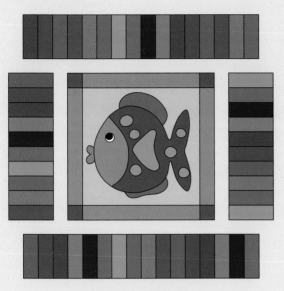

Putting it all together

FINISHING

Piping

1. Pin the flat edge of the piping to the edge of the pillow front, starting at the middle of the bottom, leaving a 1½″ end of the piping free. Pin all around, clipping into the corners.

Clip.

Leave 1½″ free.

Sewing on piping

2. Using a zipper foot, machine baste close to the cord all around. When you reach the starting point, hold the free ends of the piping together, and let them curve off the pillow's edge, and stitch down. Trim the piping ends even with the seam allowance.

Pillow Back

1. Fold under ¼″ along one long edge of each pillow back rectangle, and press. Fold under another ¼″, and press again. Topstitch in place.

2. Place the pillow front right side up, and with right sides together, place the pillow back pieces on the pillow front with the raw edges matching and the hemmed edges overlapping in the middle. Using a zipper foot, sew on the basting line around the outside edges.

3. Trim the corners, and turn the pillow cover right side out. Place the pillow form inside the pillow cover through the opening in the back.

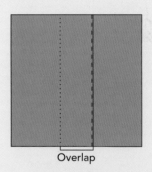

Overlap

Pillow back

turtle soft picture

MATERIALS

- ¼ yard light turquoise for appliqué block background

- ¼ yard total assorted jewel tones for appliqué pieces and pieced border

- Scrap of white for eyes

- 10½″ × 10½″ blue for back

- 10½″ × 10½″ batting

- ¼ yard paper-backed fusible web

- ½ yard ⅞″-wide lavender grosgrain ribbon for hanger

- Black permanent fabric marker or embroidery floss for eyes

Finished soft picture size: 10″ × 10″

CUTTING

Cut 1 square 6½″ × 6½″ from light turquoise for appliqué block background.

Cut the following from assorted jewel tones:

    1 strip 2½″ × 6½″ for border 1

    1 strip 2½″ × 8½″ for border 2

    1 strip 2½″ × 8½″ for border 3

    1 strip 2½″ × 10½″ for border 4

Cut 1 piece 15″ long from ribbon.

APPLIQUÉ

Refer to Appliqué on page 5.

1. Copy the turtle pattern at 75% size. Trace and cut out the reduced appliqué pieces (#1–#13). (The appliqué pattern is on page 38).

2. Appliqué the appropriate pieces onto the background. (Refer to the Turtle block diagram on page 24.)

Refer to the directions in Piecing and Putting It All Together on page 12 to finish the soft picture.

starfish security blankie

MATERIALS

- ½ yard light turquoise Flurr for blankie
- ½ yard medium turquoise flannel for binding
- ¼ yard turquoise for starfish
- Scrap of white for eyes
- Scrap of black for mouth
- ¼ yard paper-backed fusible web
- Black permanent fabric marker or embroidery floss for eyes
- Template plastic (optional)

CUTTING

Cut 1 square 18″ × 18″ from turquoise Flurr for blankie.

Refer to Cutting on page 13 for corners and binding.

APPLIQUÉ

Refer to Appliqué on page 5.

1. Copy the starfish pattern at 75% size. Trace and cut out the reduced appliqué pieces (#1–#3). (The appliqué pattern is on page 32.)

2. Appliqué the starfish onto the blankie.

3. Draw or embroider the pupils in the eyes.

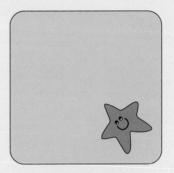

Appliqué starfish.

Refer to the directions in Putting It All Together on page 13 to finish the blankie.

Finished blankie size: 18″ × 18″

frog bib

MATERIALS

- ⅓ yard white terry cloth for bib
- ¼ yard green for frog
- Scrap of purple for tongue
- Scrap of white for eyes
- Scrap of black for mouth
- ¼ yard green for bias binding or 1 package purchased bias tape
- ¼ yard paper-backed fusible web
- 1″ × 2″ piece sew-in hook-and-loop tape
- Black permanent fabric marker or embroidery floss for frog eyes
- Template plastic (optional)

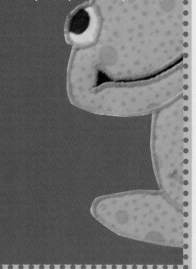

Finished bib size: 8″ × 11½″

CUTTING

Copy the bib pattern, and flip it over to make both halves of the bib. (The pattern is on the pullout.) Make a template of the complete bib. Place the template on the terry cloth. Mark and cut the bib background.

If you are making bias binding, cut bias strips 1¼″ wide from the green, and piece them end-to-end as necessary to make 49″ of bias binding.

APPLIQUÉ

Refer to Appliqué on page 5.

1. Copy the frog pattern at 75% size. Trace and cut out the reduced appliqué pieces (#1–#5). (The appliqué pattern is on page 35.)

2. Appliqué the frog onto the bib.

3. Draw or embroider the pupils in the eyes.

Appliqué frog onto bib.

Refer to the directions in Putting It All Together on page 14 to finish the bib.

Jellyfish

Starfish

Snail

Octopus

3

2

1

4

5

Frog

Sea horse

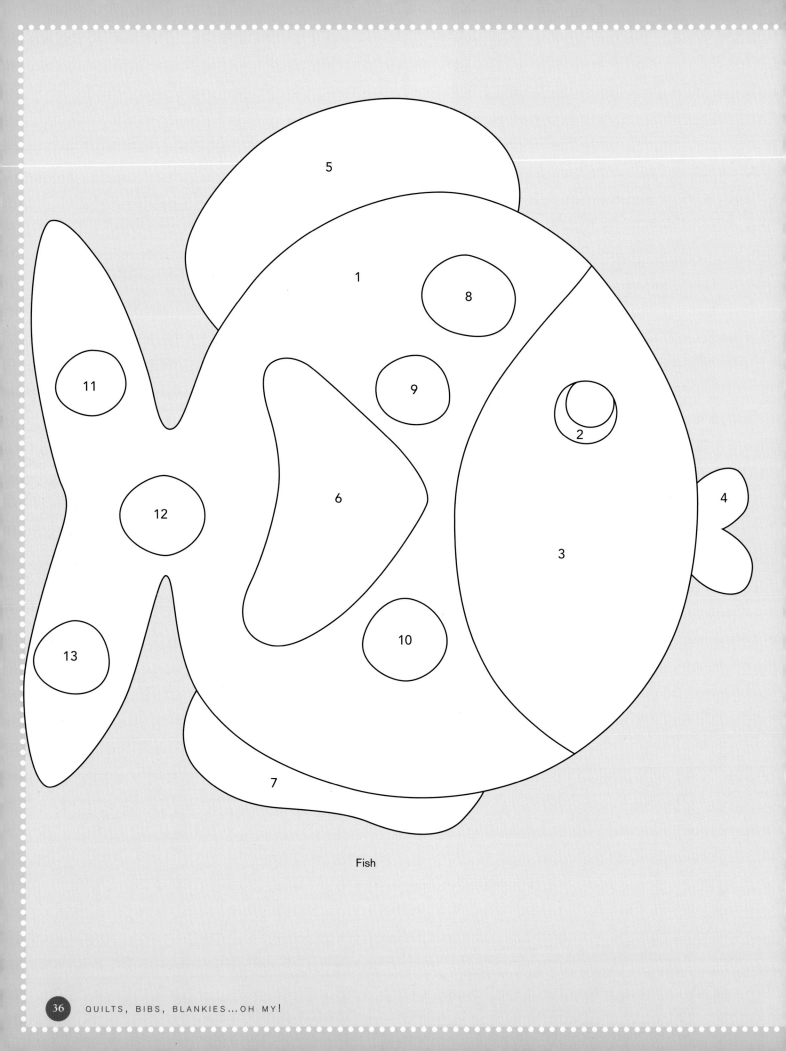

Fish

Crab

Turtle

Bring the fun and excitement of the zoo into the nursery with the projects featured in the *Zoo Parade* collection. Friendly animals decorate the *Zoo Parade* crib quilt, a giraffe growth chart, the *Zoo Parade* soft picture totem pole, a giraffe security blankie, and a lion bib.

zoo parade crib quilt

Quilted by Lynn Helmke

Finished block size: 12″ × 12″
Finished crib quilt size: 48½″ × 72½″

CUTTING

Cut 68 squares 4½″ × 4½″ from assorted medium greens for pieced blocks and pieced border.

Cut 60 squares 4½″ × 4½″ from light green for pieced blocks and pieced border.

Cut 7 squares 12½″ × 12½″ from light dots for appliqué block backgrounds.

Cut 4 strips 2½″ wide from medium green; diagonally piece the strips end-to-end as necessary (refer to page 6). Cut into 2 strips 2½″ × 60½″ for side inner borders.

Cut 2 strips 2½″ × 40½″ from medium green for top and bottom inner borders.

APPLIQUÉ

Refer to Appliqué on page 5.

1. Trace and cut out the animal appliqué pieces. (The appliqué patterns are on the pullout). Make 1 of each animal.

2. Appliqué the appropriate pieces onto the backgrounds.

3. Draw or embroider the pupils in the eyes.

Bear block, make 1.

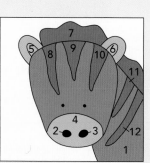

Monkey block, make 1.

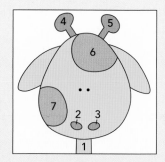

Lion block, make 1.

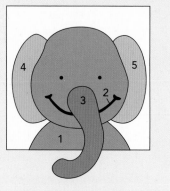

Elephant block, make 1.

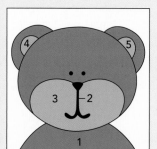

Tiger block, make 1.

Zebra block, make 1.

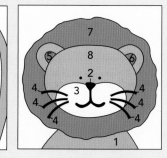

Giraffe block, make 1.

PIECING THE NINE-PATCH BLOCKS

Use 5 medium green squares and 4 light green squares for the Nine-Patch blocks. Sew 3 squares into rows as shown, and press toward the medium squares. Sew the rows into a block, and press.

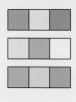

Piece blocks, make 8.

PUTTING IT ALL TOGETHER

Refer to the diagram at right.

Blocks

1. Arrange and sew together the blocks in 5 rows of 3 blocks each. Press.

2. Sew together the rows to form the block section of the quilt top. Press.

Inner Border

1. Sew the side inner borders to the quilt top. Press toward the borders.

2. Sew the top and bottom inner borders to the quilt top. Press toward the borders.

Pieced Border

1. Sew together 2 rows of 16 assorted light and medium green squares $4\frac{1}{2}'' \times 4\frac{1}{2}''$ to form the 2 side borders.

2. Sew the side borders to the quilt top, and press toward the inner border.

3. Sew together 2 rows of 12 assorted light and medium green squares $4\frac{1}{2}'' \times 4\frac{1}{2}''$ to form the top and bottom borders. Press.

4. Sew the top and bottom borders to the quilt top, and press toward the inner border.

Finishing

1. Layer the quilt with batting and backing, and baste or pin.

2. Quilt as desired, and bind.

Putting it all together

giraffe growth chart

CUTTING

Cut 1 rectangle 12½″ × 40½″ from light blue for background.

Cut 108 squares 1½″ × 1½″ from assorted brights for pieced border.

APPLIQUÉ

Refer to Appliqué on page 5.

1. Copy and join together section A to section B of the Giraffe Growth Chart pattern on the pullout. Trace and cut out the appliqué pieces.

2. Appliqué the appropriate pieces onto the background.

3. Draw or embroider the eyes.

PUTTING IT ALL TOGETHER

Refer to the diagram below.

Pieced Border

1. Sew together 2 rows of 40 squares 1½″ × 1½″ for the 2 side borders. Press.

2. Sew the 2 side borders to the growth chart, and press toward the center.

3. Sew together 2 rows of 14 squares 1½″ × 1½″ for the top and bottom borders. Press.

4. Sew the top and bottom borders to the growth chart, and press.

Putting it all together

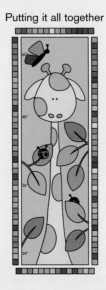

Quilted by Lynn Helmke

Finished growth chart size:
14½″ × 42½″

Finishing

1. Use a ruler to measure, and write or embroider the numbers at the side of the chart. (Refer to the photo above.)

2. Layer the growth chart with batting and backing, and baste or pin.

3. Quilt as desired, and bind.

4. Hang the chart so that the 24″ measurement is 24″ from the floor.

zoo parade
soft picture totem pole

MATERIALS

- ⅜ yard light dot for appliqué block backgrounds

- 1 yard total assorted greens for pieced borders and soft picture backs

- ½ yard total assorted brights for appliqué pieces

- ⅛ yard white for tiger muzzle

- ⅛ yard black for mouths

- 1¼ yards ⅝″-wide green grosgrain ribbon for hangers

- 5 squares 10½″ × 10½″ batting (1 per soft picture)

- 17 buttons (⅝″–1 1/16″ size)

- Black permanent fabric marker or embroidery floss for eyes

APPLIQUÉ

Refer to Appliqué on page 5.

1. Copy the bear, giraffe head, elephant and trunk, tiger, and monkey and tail patterns on the pullout at 50% size. Trace and cut out the reduced appliqué pieces.

2. Appliqué the appropriate pieces onto the backgrounds. (Refer to the block diagrams on page 40.)

Refer to the directions in Piecing and Putting It All Together on page 12 to finish the soft pictures; omit Step 2 in Putting It All Together.

FINISHING

1. Cut 1 piece of grosgrain ribbon at 12″. Fold under each end ½″, and press. Fold the ribbon in half. Attach the ribbon to the center of the top soft picture with a button to make the ribbon hanger.

Finished soft picture size: 10″ × 10″
Finished totem pole size: 10″ × 52″

2. Cut 8 pieces of grosgrain ribbon at 3¾″. Fold under each end ½″, and press. Attach the ribbon pieces between the soft pictures with buttons.

CUTTING

Cut 5 squares 6½″ × 6½″ from light dot for appliqué block backgrounds.

Cut the following from assorted greens:

5 squares 10½″ × 10½″ for backs (1 per soft picture)

5 strips 2½″ × 6½″ for border 1

5 strips 2½″ × 8½″ for border 2

5 strips 2½″ × 8½″ for border 3

5 strips 2½″ × 10½″ for border 4

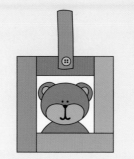

Attach ribbon hanger to top soft picture.

Attach ribbon pieces between soft pictures.

giraffe security blankie

MATERIALS

- ⅝ yard green Minkee for blankie front and back

- ½ yard green flannel for binding

- ¼ yard yellow for giraffe

- Scraps of medium yellow for giraffe spots

- Scraps of orange for giraffe knobs and nostrils

- ¼ yard paper-backed fusible web

- Template plastic (optional)

CUTTING

Cut 2 squares 18″ × 18″ from green Minkee for blankie front and back.

Refer to Cutting on page 13 for corners and binding.

APPLIQUÉ

Refer to Appliqué on page 5.

1. Copy the giraffe head pattern on the pullout at 50% size. Trace and cut out the reduced giraffe head pieces and the neck pattern piece below.

2. Appliqué the giraffe onto the blankie front.

3. Pin the blankie front to the back, wrong sides together.

Appliqué giraffe onto blankie.

Refer to the directions in Putting It All Together on page 13 to finish the blankie.

Giraffe's neck for blankie

Finished blankie size: 18″ × 18″

lion bib

Finished bib size: $8'' \times 11\frac{1}{2}''$

MATERIALS

- ⅓ yard white terry cloth for bib

- ¼ yard yellow for lion

- ¼ yard orange for lion mane

- ⅛ yard white for muzzle

- ⅛ yard black for whiskers, nose, and mouth

- ¼ yard paper-backed fusible web

- ¼ yard yellow for bias binding or 1 package of purchased bias tape

- 1″ × 2″ piece sew-in hook-and-loop tape

- Black permanent fabric marker or embroidery floss for eyes

- Template plastic (optional)

APPLIQUÉ

Refer to Appliqué on page 5.

1. Copy the lion pattern at 50% size. Trace and cut out the reduced appliqué pieces. (The appliqué pattern is on the pullout.)

2. Appliqué the lion onto the bib.

Appliqué lion.

Refer to the directions in Putting It All Together on page 14 to finish the bib.

CUTTING

Copy the bib pattern, and flip it over to make both halves of the bib. (The pattern is on the pullout.) Make a template of the complete bib. Place the template on the terry cloth. Mark and cut the background.

If you are making bias binding, cut bias strips 1¼″ wide from the yellow, and piece them end-to-end as necessary to make 49″ of bias binding.

Your new baby girl will love the sweet projects in this collection. Included are the *Somebunny Loves Me Crib Quilt*, the Hugs and Kisses pillow, the Girls Rule, Boys Drool crib or door hanger, a Bunny security blankie, and a Bunny bib.

somebunny loves me crib quilt

Quilted by Lynn Helmke

Finished crib quilt size: $48\frac{1}{2}'' \times 48\frac{1}{2}''$

CUTTING

Cut the following from light yellow:

1 square 16½″ × 16½″ for center block background

4 squares 4½″ × 4½″ for corners on outer pieced border

2 strips 2½″ × 32½″ for third border sides

2 strips 2½″ × 36½″ for third border top and bottom

36 squares 2⅞″ × 2⅞″; cut squares on the diagonal to yield 72 triangles for fourth pieced border (refer to page 5)

Cut 10 squares 4½″ × 4½″ from assorted yellows for appliqué backgrounds.

Cut the following from assorted pinks:

50 squares 4½″ × 4½″ for appliqué block backgrounds and outer pieced border

9 squares 5¼″ × 5¼″ for fourth pieced border; cut squares diagonally twice to yield 36 triangles (refer to page 5)

4 squares 2⅞″ × 2⅞″ for fourth pieced border; cut squares on the diagonal to yield 8 triangles

Cut the following from pink stripe:

2 strips 4½″ × 24½″ for second border sides

2 strips 4½″ × 32½″ for second border top and bottom

APPLIQUÉ

Refer to Appliqué on page 5.

1. Copy the bunny pattern on page 52 at 215% size. Trace and cut out the enlarged bunny pieces, as well as the hugs and kisses. You will need 1 bunny, 10 kisses, 5 hugs, and 5 reverse hugs. (Appliqué patterns are on pages 52–53.)

2. Appliqué the appropriate pieces onto the backgrounds.

3. Draw or embroider the face on the bunny.

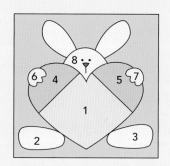

Appliqué center block.

Appliqué hugs, make 5 and make 5 reverse.

Appliqué kisses, make 10.

PUTTING IT ALL TOGETHER

Refer to the diagram on page 48.

Appliquéd Pieced Border

1. Sew together 2 rows of 4 hugs and kisses blocks for the 2 side borders. Press.

2. Sew the side borders to the quilt top, and press toward the center.

3. Sew together 2 rows of 6 hugs and kisses blocks for the top and bottom borders. Press.

4. Sew the top and bottom borders to the quilt top, and press.

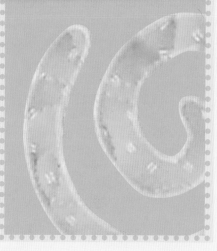

Second Border

1. Sew the pink stripe second side border strips to the quilt top, and press toward the second border.

2. Sew the pink stripe second top and bottom border strips to the quilt top, and press toward the second border.

Third Border

1. Sew the light yellow third side border strips to the quilt top, and press toward the second border.

2. Sew the light yellow third top and bottom border strips to the quilt top, and press toward the second border.

Fourth Pieced Border

1. Sew 2 light yellow triangles to 1 pink triangle on the diagonal edges. Press Make 32 blocks.

Sew triangles, make 32 blocks.

2. Arrange and sew 4 rows of 8 blocks to form the borders. Press.

3. Sew together a light yellow triangle and a pink triangle on the diagonal edges for the side borders. Press. Make 4 units.

Sew triangles, make 4.

4. Sew a unit from Step 3 to each end of the side borders. Press.

Add units to side borders.

5. Sew the side borders to the quilt top, and press toward the third border.

6. Sew 1 pink and 1 yellow small triangle to a large pink triangle on the diagonal edges for the top and bottom borders. Press. Make 2.

Sew triangles, make 2.

7. Sew 1 pink and 1 yellow small triangle to a large pink triangle on the diagonal edges to make a mirror image of the unit made in Step 6. Press. Make 2.

Sew triangles, make 2.

8. Sew the units from Steps 6 and 7 to each end of the top and bottom borders. Press.

Add units to top and bottom borders.

9. Sew the top and bottom borders to the quilt top, and press toward the third border.

Outer Pieced Border

1. Sew together 4 rows of 10 squares 4½″ × 4½″ from the assorted pinks for the outer borders. Press.

> ### NOTE
> To match the look of the quilt on page 46, arrange the pinks to match the order of the pinks in the fourth pieced border.

2. Sew the 2 side borders to the quilt top, and press toward the outer border.

3. Sew a yellow square 4½″ × 4½″ to each end of the remaining rows for the top and bottom borders. Press.

4. Sew the top and bottom borders to the quilt top, and press toward the outer border.

Finishing

1. Layer the quilt with batting and backing, and baste or pin.

2. Quilt as desired, and bind.

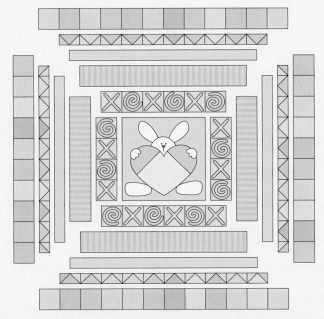

Putting it all together

hugs and kisses pillow

Finished pillow size: 18″ × 18″

MATERIALS

- ¼ yard total assorted yellows for appliqué block backgrounds, appliqué pieces, and pieced borders

- ½ yard total assorted pinks for appliqué block backgrounds, appliqué pieces, and pieced borders

- ⅝ yard pink for pillow back

- 2¼ yards purchased pink piping

- ⅛ yard paper-backed fusible web

- Pink permanent fabric marker or embroidery floss for face

- 18″ × 18″ pillow form

CUTTING

Cut the following from assorted yellows:
2 squares 4½″ × 4½″ for appliqué block backgrounds

8 squares 2⅞″ × 2⅞″ for inner pieced border; cut squares on the diagonal to yield 16 triangles (refer to page 5)

4 squares 2½″ × 2½″ for corners of inner pieced border

Cut the following from assorted pinks:
2 squares 4½″ × 4½″ for appliqué block backgrounds

2 squares 5¼″ × 5¼″ for inner pieced border; cut squares diagonally twice to yield 8 triangles (refer to page 5)

20 squares 3½″ × 3½″ for outer pieced border

Cut 2 rectangles 12½″ × 18½″ from pink for back.

APPLIQUÉ

Refer to Appliqué on page 5.

1. Trace and cut out 1 hug, 1 reverse hug, and 2 kisses appliqué pieces (#9–#10). (Appliqué patterns are on page 53.)

2. Appliqué the appropriate pieces onto the background.

Appliqué hugs, make 1 and make 1 reverse.

Appliqué kisses, make 2.

PUTTING IT ALL TOGETHER

Refer to the diagram on at right.

Piecing

1. Sew together 2 rows of 2 hugs and kisses blocks for the center block. Press.

2. Sew together the rows to form the center block. Press.

Inner Pieced Border

1. Sew 2 yellow triangles to 1 pink triangle on the diagonal edges. (Refer to the diagram on page 48.) Press. Make 8.

2. Arrange and sew together 4 rows of 2 blocks each to form the borders. Press.

3. Sew the side borders to the pillow top, and press toward the border.

4. Sew a yellow 2½″ × 2½″ square to each end of the remaining rows for the top and bottom borders. Press.

5. Sew the top and bottom borders to the pillow top, and press toward the border.

Outer Pieced Border

1. Arrange and sew together 2 rows of 4 squares 3½″ × 3½″ from the assorted pinks for the 2 side borders.

2. Sew the side borders to the pillow top, and press toward the outer border.

3. Arrange and sew together 2 rows of 6 squares 3½″ × 3½″ from the assorted pinks for the top and bottom borders. Press.

4. Sew the top and bottom borders to the pillow top, and press toward the outer border.

Refer to the directions in Finishing on page 27 to complete the pillow.

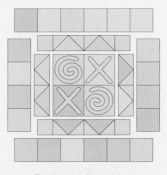

Putting it all together

girls rule, boys drool crib or door hanger

MATERIALS

- ⅛ yard total assorted pinks for center block and hearts
- ⅛ yard total assorted yellows for borders
- 10½″ × 10½″ pink for hanger back
- ⅛ yard paper-backed fusible web
- 1⅜ yards ⅞″-wide pink grosgrain ribbon for hanger
- Polyester fiberfill
- Dark pink permanent fabric marker or embroidery floss for lettering

CUTTING

Cut 3 rectangles 2½″ × 6½″ from assorted pinks for center block.

Cut the following from assorted yellows:

    1 strip 2½″ × 6½″ for border 1
    1 strip 2½″ × 8½″ for border 2
    1 strip 2½″ × 8½″ for border 3
    1 strip 2½″ × 10½″ for border 4

Cut 2 pieces 24″ long from ribbon.

PIECING

1. Sew together the 3 pink rectangles to form the center block. Press.

2. Follow the border sequence numbers, and sew the borders to the center block clockwise, pressing toward the border after each addition. (Refer to the diagram on page 11.)

Finished block size: 6″ × 6″

Finished hanger size: 10″ × 10″

APPLIQUÉ

Refer to Appliqué on page 5.

1. Trace and cut out 3 hearts. (The appliqué pattern is on page 53.)

2. Appliqué the appropriate pieces onto the hanger.

3. Use the pink permanent marker or embroidery floss for the lettering. (The pattern is on page 53.)

Appliqué hearts and add lettering.

Refer to the directions in Putting It All Together on page 11 to complete the hanger.

bunny security blankie

MATERIALS

- ⅝ yard pink Flurr for blankie
- ½ yard pink dot flannel for binding
- ⅛ yard light for bunny
- ⅛ yard total of 2 pinks for heart
- ⅛ yard paper-backed fusible web
- Dark pink permanent fabric marker or embroidery floss for face
- Template plastic (optional)

CUTTING

Cut 1 square 18″ × 18″ from pink Flurr for blankie.

Refer to Cutting on page 13 for corners and binding.

APPLIQUÉ

Refer to Appliqué on page 5.

1. Trace and cut out 1 each of the bunny pieces (#1–#8). (The appliqué pattern is on page 52.)

2. Appliqué the bunny and heart onto the blankie.

Finished blankie size: 18″ × 18″

Appliqué bunny and heart.

3. Draw or embroider the face on the bunny.

Follow the directions in Putting It All Together on page 13 to finish the blankie.

bunny bib

CUTTING

Copy the bib pattern, and flip it over to make both halves of the bib. (The pattern is on the pullout.) Make a template of the complete bib. Place the template on the terry cloth. Mark and cut the bib background.

If you are making bias binding, cut bias strips 1¼″ wide from the pink satin, and piece them end-to-end as necessary to make 49″ of bias binding.

Finished bib size: 8″ × 11½″

MATERIALS

- ⅓ yard white terry cloth for bib
- ⅛ yard light for bunny
- ⅛ yard total of 2 pinks for heart
- ¼ yard pink satin for bias binding or 1 package purchased bias tape
- ¼ yard paper-backed fusible web
- 1″ × 2″ piece sew-in hook-and-loop tape
- Dark pink permanent fabric marker or embroidery floss for face
- Template plastic (optional)

APPLIQUÉ

Refer to Appliqué on page 5.

1. Trace and cut out 1 each of the bunny and heart pieces (#1–#8). (The appliqué pattern is below.)

2. Appliqué the bunny and heart onto the bib.

3. Draw or embroider the face.

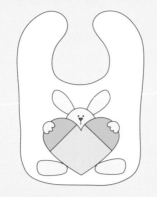

Appliqué bunny and heart onto bib.

Refer to the directions in Putting It All Together on page 14 to finish the bib.

Bunny

10

9

Kiss

Hug

Girls Rule
Boys Drool

Heart

Saying

For the first few weeks of their lives, babies can see only black and white. Stimulate their imagination and development with the *Counting Sheep* collection featuring black and white fabrics. The sheepish collection includes a crib quilt, growth chart, soft picture, security blankie, and bib.

counting sheep crib quilt

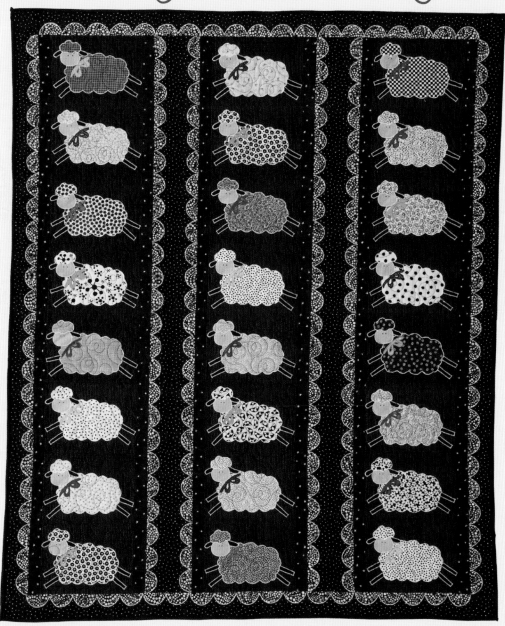

Quilted by Lynn Helmke

Finished block size: 8˝ × 6˝

Finished crib quilt size: 42½˝ × 52½˝

CUTTING

Cut 24 rectangles 8½″ × 6½″ from black print for appliqué block backgrounds.

Cut the following from black dot:

16 rectangles 4½″ × 6½″ for appliquéd scallop backgrounds

16 rectangles 2½″ × 6½″ for appliquéd scallop backgrounds

6 rectangles 2½″ × 10½″ for appliquéd scallop backgrounds

4 rectangles 2½″ × 4½″ for appliquéd scallop backgrounds

4 squares 2½″ × 2½″ for corners

Cut 6 strips 1½″ × 48½″ lengthwise from black star.

APPLIQUÉ

Refer to Appliqué on page 5.

1. Trace and cut out 24 each of the sheep pattern pieces (#1–#5). Trace and cut out 96 legs (#6), 48 vertical scallop pieces (#7), 6 top and bottom border scallop pieces (#8), and 4 top and bottom border scallop pieces (#9). (Appliqué patterns are on pages 61–62.)

2. Appliqué the appropriate pieces onto each background.

3. Draw or embroider the eyes on the sheep.

Appliqué sheep, make 24.

Appliqué scallop sashing sections, make 16.

Appliqué scallop side border sections, make 16.

Appliqué scallop top and bottom border sections, make 6.

Appliqué scallop top and bottom border sections, make 4.

PUTTING IT ALL TOGETHER

Refer to the diagram on page 56.

Arrange and sew together 3 columns of 8 sheep blocks for the sheep section. Press.

Vertical Sashing

Sew a sashing strip to each side of the sheep columns. Press toward the sashing.

Pieced Scallop Sashing

1. Sew together 2 rows of 8 scallop sashing sections. Press.

2. Sew the scallop sashing sections between the sheep columns. Press toward the vertical sashing.

MATERIALS

- 1⅓ yards black print for appliqué block backgrounds

- 3¼ yards black star for vertical sashing and backing

- 1 yard black dot for scallop backgrounds and corners

- 1 yard total assorted black-and-white prints for sheep

- ⅓ yard black for legs and ears

- ⅛ yard total assorted brights for bows

- ⅛ yard pink for faces

- ¾ yard black-and-white print for scallops

- ½ yard for binding

- 3 yards paper-backed fusible web

- 46″ × 56″ batting

- Black permanent fabric marker or embroidery floss for faces

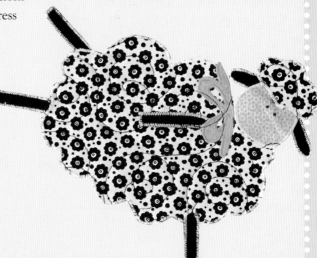

Pieced Scallop Border

1. Sew together 2 rows of 8 scallop border sections for the 2 side borders. Press.

2. Sew the 2 side borders to the quilt top. Press toward the border.

3. Sew 2 border corners, 3 five-scallop border sections, and 2 two-scallop border sections in a row to make the top border. Press. Sew the border to the quilt, and press. Repeat for the bottom border.

Piece top and bottom borders, make 2.

4. Sew the top and bottom borders to the quilt top. Press toward the border.

Finishing

1. Layer the quilt with batting and backing, and baste or pin.

2. Quilt as desired, and bind.

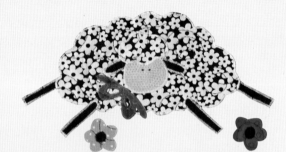

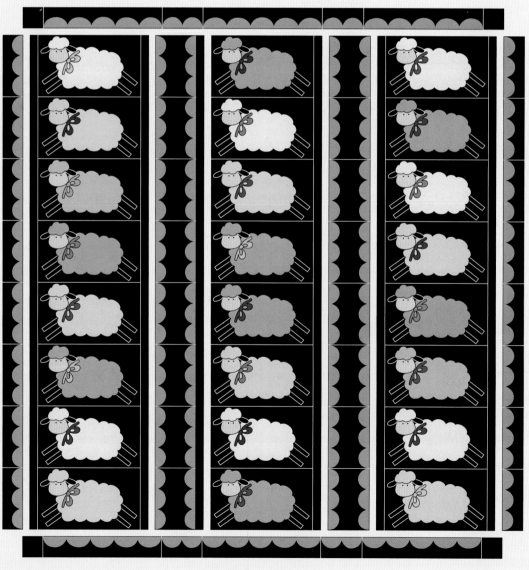

Putting it all together

pile of sheep growth chart

MATERIALS

- ½ yard black dot for appliqué background
- ⅛ yard pink for sheep faces
- ¼ yard black for legs, ears, and flower centers
- ⅜ yard total assorted black-and-white prints for sheep
- Scraps of assorted brights for bows, butterflies, sun, and flowers
- ⅛ yard green for grass
- ¼ yard white for appliquéd scallop border
- ⅓ yard black star for scallop border background
- 1⅝ yards for backing and binding
- 1¾ yards paper-backed fusible web
- 22″ × 44″ batting
- Black permanent fabric marker or embroidery floss for eyes and numbers

CUTTING

Cut 1 rectangle 12½″ × 40½″ from black dot for appliqué background.

Cut 2 strips 3½″ × 40½″ from black star for appliquéd scallop border background.

APPLIQUÉ

Refer to Appliqué on page 5.

1. Trace and cut out the appliqué pieces. Make 2 open butterflies, 5 flowers, and 10 scallop pieces. Make 1 of each of the rest of the pieces. (The appliqué patterns are on the pullout.)

2. Appliqué the appropriate pieces onto the backgrounds. (Refer to the photo and the diagram.)

3. Draw or embroider the eyes on the sheep.

PUTTING IT ALL TOGETHER

Refer to the diagram below.

Borders

1. Sew a scallop border piece to each side of the appliquéd center. Press toward the center.

2. Use a ruler to measure and write or embroider the numbers at the side of the chart.

Quilted by Lynn Helmke

Finished size: 18½″ × 40½″

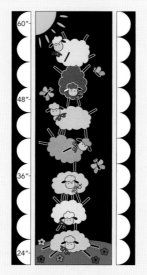

Putting it all together

Finishing

1. Layer the growth chart with batting and backing, and baste or pin.

2. Quilt as desired, and bind.

3. Hang the chart so that the 24″ measurement is 24″ from the floor.

sheep soft picture

MATERIALS

- ⅓ yard black star for appliqué block background and picture back

- ¼ yard total assorted black-and-white prints for borders and sheep

- Scrap of black for ears and legs

- Scrap of pink for face

- Scrap of red for bow

- ¼ yard paper-backed fusible web

- ½ yard ⅞″-wide black or red grosgrain ribbon for hanger

- 10½″ × 10½″ batting

- Black permanent fabric marker or embroidery floss for eyes

CUTTING

Cut the following from black star:

1 square 6½″ × 6½″ for appliqué block background

1 square 10½″ × 10½″ for back

Cut the following from assorted black-and-white prints:

1 strip 2½″ × 6½″ for border 1

1 strip 2½″ × 8½″ for border 2

1 strip 2½″ × 8½″ for border 3

1 strip 2½″ × 10½″ for border 4

Cut 1 piece 15″ long from ribbon.

PIECING

Follow the border sequence numbers, and sew the borders onto the appliqué block clockwise, pressing toward the border after each addition. (Refer to Piecing layout on page 12.)

APPLIQUÉ

Refer to Appliqué on page 5.

1. Trace and cut out 1 each of the sheep pieces (#1–#5). Cut out 4 legs (#6). (Appliqué patterns are on page 61.)

2. Appliqué the appropriate pieces onto the soft picture.

3. Draw or embroider the eyes on the sheep.

Appliqué layout

Refer to the directions in Putting It All Together on page 12 to finish the soft picture.

Finished soft picture size: 10″ × 10″

sheep security blankie

MATERIALS

- ⅝ yard black dot flannel for appliqué background and blankie back

- ½ yard black star flannel for binding

- ⅓ yard gray flannel for border

- ¼ yard white-and-black flannel for scallops

- ⅛ yard black-and-white print for sheep

- Scrap of black for ears and legs

- Scrap of pink for face

- Scrap of red for bow

- ⅓ yard paper-backed fusible web

- Black permanent fabric marker or embroidery floss for eyes

- Template plastic (optional)

CUTTING

Cut the following from black dot flannel:

1 square 12½″ × 12½″ for appliqué background

1 square 18½″ × 18½″ for back

Cut the following from gray flannel:

2 strips 3½″ × 12½″ for scallop border backgrounds

2 strips 3½″ × 18½″ for scallop border backgrounds.

APPLIQUÉ

Refer to Appliqué on page 5.

1. Trace and cut out 1 each of the sheep pieces (#1–#5). Cut out 4 legs (#6). (Appliqué patterns are on page 61.) Cut out 4 scallop pieces (#10). (The pattern is on the pullout.)

2. Appliqué the appropriate pieces onto the backgrounds.

3. Draw or embroider the eyes on the sheep.

Appliqué blankie.

Finished blankie size: 18½″ × 18½″

PUTTING IT ALL TOGETHER

1. Sew the side borders onto the appliquéd background square. Press toward the border. Repeat for the top and bottom borders.

2. Layer the blankie front and back wrong sides together, and pin.

3. Refer to Cutting on page 13 for corners and binding.

Refer to the directions in Putting It All Together on page 13 to finish the blankie.

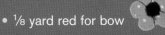 # sheep bib

Finished bib size: $8'' \times 11\frac{1}{2}''$

MATERIALS

- ⅓ yard white terry cloth for bib

- ⅙ yard black print for sheep

- ⅛ yard pink for face

- ⅛ yard red for bow

- ⅛ yard black for legs and ears

- ¼ yard black-and-white check for bias binding or 1 package of purchased bias tape

- ¼ yard paper-backed fusible web

- 1″ × 2″ piece sew-in hook-and-loop tape

- Black permanent fabric marker or embroidery floss for eyes

- Template plastic (optional)

CUTTING

Copy the bib pattern, and flip it over to make both sides of the bib. (The pattern is on the pullout.) Make a template of the complete bib. Place the template on the terry cloth. Mark and cut the bib background.

If you are making bias binding, cut bias strips 1¼″ wide from the black-and-white check, and piece them end-to-end as necessary to make 49″ of bias binding.

APPLIQUÉ

Refer to Appliqué on page 5.

1. Trace and cut out 1 each of the sheep pieces (#1–#5). Cut out 4 legs (#6) (Appliqué patterns are on page 61.)

2. Appliqué the sheep onto the bib.

3. Draw or embroider the eyes.

Appliqué sheep onto bib.

Refer to the directions in Putting It All Together on page 14 to finish the bib.

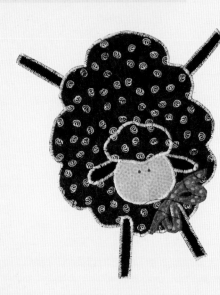

Sheep

Side scallop

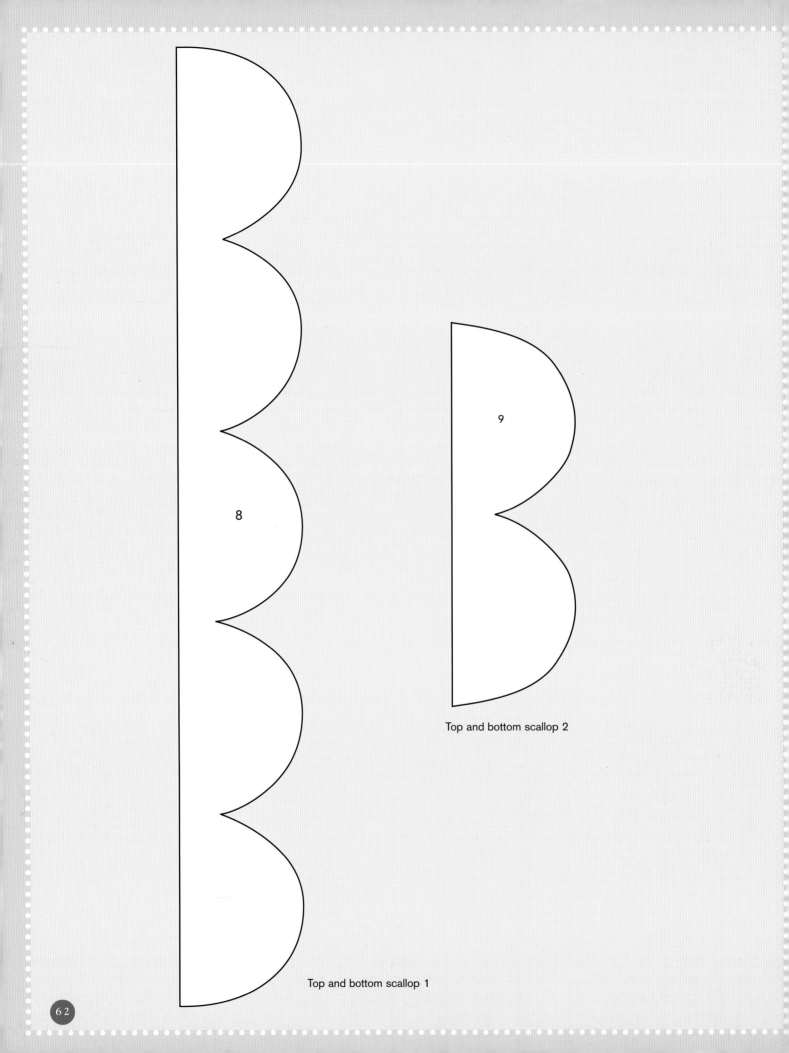

8

9

Top and bottom scallop 2

Top and bottom scallop 1

about the author

Kim Schaefer is from southeastern Wisconsin, where she lives with her husband, Gary, her sons, Max, Ben, Sam, and Gator, and her dog, Rio—all of whom she lovingly refers to as the "Neanderthals." Kim and Gary also have two daughters, Cody and Ali. Cody lives nearby, and Ali attends college in Minnesota. Kim's stepsons, Gary Jr. and Dax, also live nearby, and her stepdaughters, Tina and Danielle, live in Phoenix.

Kim began sewing at an early age, which Kim says was a nightmare for her mom, who continually, and patiently, untangled bobbin messes. Kim was formally educated at the University of Wisconsin in Milwaukee, where she studied fine arts and majored in fiber. At age 23, Kim took her first quilting class and was immediately hooked.

In 1996, Little Quilt Company was born and made its debut at Quilt Market in Minneapolis. In addition to designing quilt patterns, Kim designs fabric for Andover/Makower and works with Leo Licensing, who licenses her designs for nonfabric products.

Other books by Kim Schaefer

resources

FOR A LIST OF OTHER FINE BOOKS FROM C&T PUBLISHING, ASK FOR A FREE CATALOG:

C&T Publishing, Inc.
P.O. Box 1456
Lafayette, CA 94549
(800) 284-1114
Email: ctinfo@ctpub.com
Website: www.ctpub.com

For quilting supplies:

Cotton Patch
1025 Brown Ave.
Lafayette, CA 94549
(800) 835-4418 or
(925) 283-7883
Email: CottonPa@aol.com
Website: www.quiltusa.com

Note: Fabrics used in the quilts shown may not be currently available, as fabric manufacturers keep most fabrics in print for only a short time.

C&T Publishing's professional photography services are now available to the public.
Visit us at www.ctmediaservices.com.

Great Titles from C&T PUBLISHING